Dragonflies

Leo Statts

abdopublishing.com

Published by Abdo Zoom™, PO Box 398166, Minneapolis, Minnesota 55439. Copyright © 2017 by Abdo Consulting Group, Inc. International copyrights reserved in all countries. No part of this book may be reproduced in any form without written permission from the publisher. Abdo Zoom™ is a trademark and logo of Abdo Consulting Group, Inc.

Printed in the United States of America, North Mankato, Minnesota
062016
092016

Cover Photo: Peera Stockfoto/Shutterstock Images
Interior Photos: iStockphoto, 1, 4–5, 6, 10–11, 13, 18, 19; Areeya Ann/iStockphoto, 5; Luká Hejtman/iStockphoto, 7; Mike Bousquet/iStockphoto, 8–9; Red Line Editorial, 9, 20 (left), 20 (right), 21 (left), 21 (right); Atid Kiattisaksiri/iStockphoto, 12–13; Tian Yuan Only/iStockphoto, 14–15; Patrick Rolands/Shutterstock Images, 16; Vitalii Hulai/Shutterstock Images, 17

Editor: Brienna Rossiter
Series Designer: Madeline Berger
Art Direction: Dorothy Toth

Publisher's Cataloging-in-Publication Data
Names: Statts, Leo, author.
Title: Dragonflies / by Leo Statts.
Description: Minneapolis, MN : Abdo Zoom, [2017] | Series: Swamp animals |
    Includes bibliographical references and index.
Identifiers: LCCN 2016941191 | ISBN 9781680792096 (lib. bdg.) |
    ISBN 9781680793772 (ebook) | ISBN 9781680794663 (Read-to-me ebook)
Subjects: LCSH: Dragonflies--Juvenile literature.
Classification: DDC 595.7--dc23
LC record available at http://lccn.loc.gov/2016941191

Table of Contents

Dragonflies. 4

Body 6

Habitat 8

Food 12

Life Cycle 16

Quick Stats. 20

Glossary 22

Booklinks 23

Index 24

Dragonflies

Dragonflies are insects.

They can be many colors.
Many live near water.

Body

Dragonflies have six legs.
They have four wings.

They have two large eyes.
Some have hairy bodies.

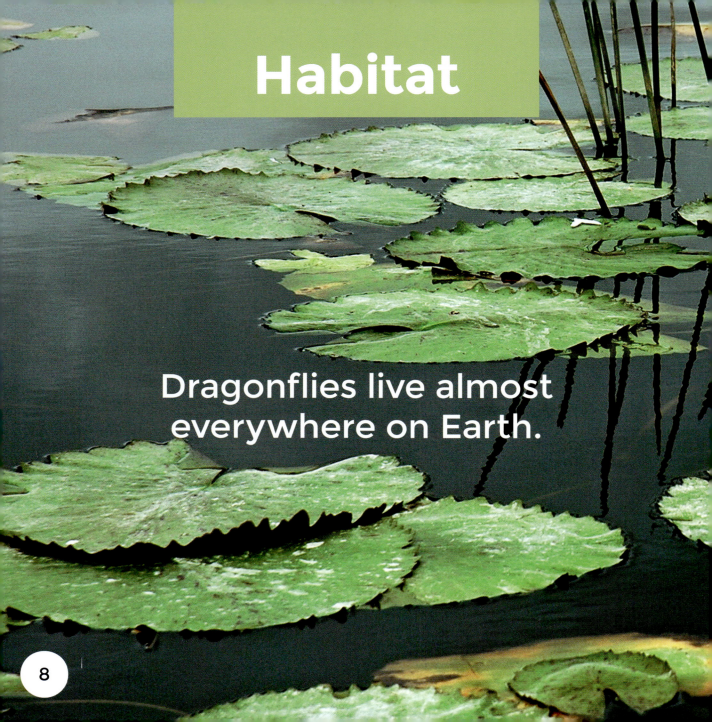

Habitat

Dragonflies live almost everywhere on Earth.

▢ Where dragonflies live

Some dragonflies live near lakes or ponds. Others live by **streams**.

They can live in **swamps**, too.

Food

Dragonflies are good hunters. It is easy for them to catch **prey**.

Dragonflies eat other insects. They often eat mosquitoes.

Flies are another common food.

Life Cycle

Dragonflies lay eggs.
Some lay hundreds of eggs.

Some lay more than a thousand. **Nymphs** later **hatch** from the eggs.

Nymphs live underwater. Some stay there for several years.

Then they become adults. Most adult dragonflies live only a few weeks.

Average Length

A dragonfly is longer than a baseball.

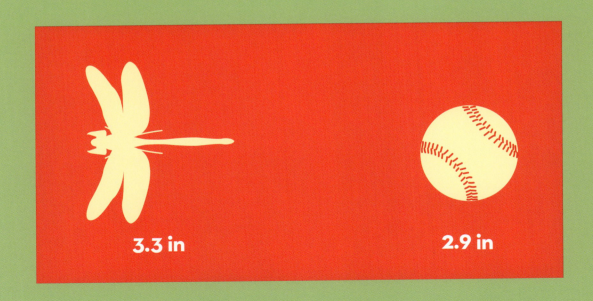

3.3 in

2.9 in

Average Wingspan

A dragonfly's wingspan is wider than a baseball.

4 in

2.9 in

Glossary

hatch - to be born from an egg.

nymph - a baby insect.

prey - an animal that is hunted and eaten by another animal.

stream - a small, flowing body of water.

swamp - wet land that is filled with trees, plants, or both.

Booklinks

For more information on **dragonflies**, please visit booklinks.abdopublishing.com

Learn even more with the Abdo Zoom Animals database. Check out **abdozoom.com** for more information.

Index

colors, 5

eggs, 16, 17

eyes, 7

food, 15

lakes, 10

legs, 6

nymphs, 17, 18

ponds, 10

streams, 10

swamps, 11

wings, 6